Longman Structural Readers: Fiction
Stage 4

Eight Ghost Stories

S. H. Burton

Illustrated by Ian Newsham

Longman

Longman Group Limited
London

*Associated companies, branches and representatives
throughout the world*

This edition © Longman Group Ltd 1979

This edition first published 1979

ISBN 0 582 54078 X

Printed in Hong Kong by
Commonwealth Printing Press Ltd

Contents

Contents

Oldcastle Hill

Mr Robinson lived in Dunpool, a small town in the West of England. He lived alone in a pretty little house in the High Street. He was wealthy, so he did not need to work. He had never married, but he was not lonely. He had a lot of books in his little house and he read a great deal. He was very fond of walking, too, and he explored the high moorland around Dunpool. Mrs Wills came to his house every day to clean it and to cook for him. She liked talking. Mr Robinson used to tell his friends that he could not be lonely while Mrs Wills worked for him.

One day in the spring, Mr Robinson was walking in the hills. The sun was shining and the birds were singing. He felt happy, as he always did when he was out among the hills. The lonely moorland filled him with pleasure. The fresh air, the quietness, the grass, the rolling hills made him glad to be alive. He was walking along a path that he had often followed. Suddenly, he noticed a track that led off to his left. 'That's strange,' he said to himself. 'I've never noticed that track before.'

He turned away from the familiar path and followed the track on his left. The track wound its way between a valley and a high hill. The valley contained a pretty little river. 'This is one of the most beautiful places I have ever seen,' Mr Robinson thought. It was very lonely, but he liked the lonely places in the moorland. He looked at his map. The high hill was marked on the map. It was called Oldcastle Hill.

After he had walked for about a mile, he came to the foot of Oldcastle Hill. He thought, 'I will climb this hill and rest at the top. There will be a good view from there.'

The hill wasn't easy to climb. Mr Robinson had to stop several times. Each time he stopped, he looked round him, and each time the country seemed wilder. 'How strange!' he thought, but he explained the effect by the fact that he was going higher and higher. When he reached the top, he looked down at the country below. He could hardly recognize it.

'I know it so well,' he thought, 'but it seems different today. Of course, I have never stood on top of this hill before. I must not be surprised that things look different from here. At least, I can see the track that leads home to Dunpool.'

He looked round. The hill top was covered with short grass. There were no trees, but a low wall ran across the middle of the ground. Mr Robinson walked up to it. It was made of earth and it was covered with grass. It stood about four feet high and seemed very old.

'Now, I wonder who built this?' Mr Robinson said to himself. He climbed over the wall and sat down on the ground. He rested his back against the wall and enjoyed the warm sun. He was so comfortable that he soon fell asleep.

When he woke, the sun was low in the sky. He stood up quickly, climbed back over the wall and began to hurry towards the Dunpool track. He did not want to be in the hills in the dark.

Mr Robinson was about halfway down the hill when he felt afraid. He knew that somebody was watching him from the hill top.

'Don't be so foolish!' he said to himself. 'Your back is turned to the hill top. How can you be so sure that somebody is watching you?' He had plenty of courage and he decided to stop and turn round. If somebody was watching him he would demand a reason.

Then suddenly Mr Robinson remembered his dream on the hill top and he did not stop. Nor did he turn round. He ran towards the Dunpool track and he did not slow down until he reached that familiar path.

During his sleep on the hill top, he dreamed he had heard voices. He had not understood them. He was unable to recognize the language. It was certainly not English. Nor did he know how many different voices he could hear. Were they men's voices or women's? He could not be sure. He was sure of nothing in his dream. But the voices seemed angry. And, in his sleep, Mr Robinson knew that the speakers were looking at him. He could not see them, but they could see him.

When he woke up, he had forgotten the dream. At that time he was thinking only of getting back to Dunpool before dark. The dream returned to his memory when those hidden eyes watched him from the hill top.

Mr Robinson walked home quickly. He had a lot to think about. There was a mystery here; and he hated mysteries.

Mrs Wills had left his supper on the table. He ate it quickly. He hardly noticed what he was eating. Then he pushed his chair back and left his dining room. He went to his desk, took out some sheets of paper and began to write. He wrote a careful report of everything that had happened at Oldcastle Hill that day. He signed the report and wrote the date at the bottom. Then he placed the report against his inkpot. There, it would be seen by anybody who went near his desk. After that, he had a drink and went to bed early. Mr Robinson had decided to solve the mystery of Oldcastle Hill.

At eleven o'clock the next morning, he was climbing slowly up the side of the hill. He moved quietly and carefully. Sometimes he stopped and stared at the empty hillside ahead of him. When he was sure that nobody was watching him he went forwards again.

At last, he reached the top. Nothing moved. Nobody spoke. The hill top was empty. He took a deep breath and began to walk towards the wall. He was now sure that the secret of Oldcastle Hill lay behind that wall. He was going to climb over the wall and solve its mystery. He was a brave man, but his heart beat quickly. He *had* to find out the cause of yesterday's fears. He *had* to climb that wall. He could never enjoy the lovely hills again if he ran away now. His steps slowed down. He stopped. His head was still, but his eyes moved from side to side. Something had moved behind the wall! He could hear voices! He must find his hidden enemy. He must not show his fear. He stood there, straight; his face towards the wall.

A small stone struck him with terrible force between the eyes. He fell without making a sound. The top of Oldcastle Hill was quiet and empty, but Mr Robinson lay dead in front of the grassy wall.

In Mr Robinson's house the next morning, Mrs Wills lifted the telephone and rang the police station.

'It's never happened before,' she said. 'He's not here, I tell you. He hasn't slept in his bed. Yes, I *am* afraid. I'm afraid that something has happened to him. Please send somebody round here at once.'

A few minutes later, a policeman knocked at the door.

'I'm glad you've come,' she said. 'Have a look at this.' She took the policeman into Mr Robinson's sitting room and showed him the sheets of paper that Mr Robinson had left on his desk.

The policeman read Mr Robinson's report slowly and carefully. Then he put the sheets of paper in his pocket. 'I'll have to keep these,' he said. 'Did you see him yesterday?'

'Yes,' Mrs Wills answered. 'But only for a few minutes. He went out quite early. I was washing his breakfast dishes when he left the house.'

'Did he seem well?'

'Oh yes. He was quiet...quieter than usual...but he wasn't ill.'

'Did he say where he was going?'

'He said that he was going walking in the hills.'

The policeman nodded. 'Yes,' he said. 'In the hills. That's not surprising. Did he say anything to you about a place called Oldcastle Hill?'

'No,' Mrs Wills answered. 'He didn't.'

The policeman put his hand in his pocket and touched the report that Mr Robinson had left on his desk.

'Well,' he said, 'I'm going to look for him on Oldcastle Hill. Poor Mr Robinson...he seemed to think he had an enemy there. I'm afraid he may have found him.'

About an hour later, the policeman and a detective found Mr Robinson's body in front of the wall on Oldcastle Hill.

'Look at that!' The policeman spoke in a low voice as he pointed at the dead man's face. 'That's terrible! Who could have done that to him?'

'I don't know *who* did it,' the detective answered. 'But I know *what* did it.' He knelt down by the body and pointed at a small round stone. It was lying in the grass by the dead man's head. He took his handkerchief out of his pocket and picked up the stone with it.

'Now,' he said, 'we must search the hill top. Somebody was up here yesterday. Somebody was waiting for Mr Robinson. There must be some marks in the grass. Look carefully for footprints. You search the righthand side and I'll search the left. Be specially careful near the wall. The killer hid there. Look for footprints leading up to it.'

They searched the top of Oldcastle Hill for more than an hour, but they found nothing. Mr Robinson's footprints were plain. They led from the Dunpool side of the hill top to the place where his body lay. There were no other footprints.

'Well, that's that!' said the detective. 'There's nothing here...nothing but a dead man and the stone that killed him. You'd better get back to Dunpool police station. We'll need help to carry the body to the road.'

The detective lit a cigarette as he sat waiting on that sunny hill top. He looked at Mr Robinson's body and he looked at the grassy wall. It was a warm spring day, but he suddenly felt cold. He stood up and threw his cigarette away. His thoughts troubled him.

'A dead man,' he said to himself. 'A small round stone. And nothing else. A killer has been at work up here on this hill top and then disappeared. Not a footprint...not a sign ...nothing to lead me to him.'

He looked down towards the Dunpool track and he was glad to see figures climbing up the hill. The detective had been alone on Oldcastle Hill long enough to be afraid.

A few days later, the detective visited the library in Oxminster, a big city not far from Dunpool. He asked to see the chief librarian.

'What can you tell me about Oldcastle Hill?' he asked.

'It was an important place many years ago,' the librarian answered.

'Important? Oldcastle Hill was important, you say?'

'Don't be so surprised. I'm talking about the ancient people who lived there more than a thousand years ago. They lived there before Oxminster or Dunpool had any inhabitants. Nobody knew about Oxminster or Dunpool then. The ancient people built the wall on the hill top. From behind that wall they beat back their enemies who tried to climb the hill.'

'I see,' the detective said, slowly. He put a small round stone on the library table. 'And what can you tell me about that?' he asked.

The librarian picked it up and looked at it carefully. 'You found this on Oldcastle Hill,' he said.

'I did. How did you know?'

'Several stones like this were found there about a hundred years ago. They were taken to the Oxminster museum. If you go to the museum they will show them to you. You'd better take this stone there. They will be glad to have it.'

'I can't do that,' said the detective. 'But why is this stone so special? Why would they like to have it in the museum?'

'It belonged to the ancient people,' the librarian answered. 'Their fighting men used these stones and they could throw them with terrible effect. I tell you, these stones were as dangerous as bullets. In ancient days many men were killed on Oldcastle Hill with stones like this in their heads.'

The detective said nothing. He got up and put the stone back in his pocket.

'I hope I've been able to help you?' the librarian asked.

'You've been very interesting,' the detective said. 'But I'm afraid that you haven't been able to solve my problem. I am a policeman. I am looking for a killer. It is my duty to find him. I cannot explain that Mr Robinson's killer died more than a thousand years ago.'

Room 7

I didn't tell this story to anybody for many years. I couldn't explain the mystery and I thought that people wouldn't believe me. It doesn't matter so much to me now if I'm not believed. I'm telling a true story. You may not believe in ghosts. I'm not sure that I believe in them. I'm not sure that I saw a ghost that night. If I didn't see a ghost, I don't know what I saw.

I'd been on a business trip to the north of England and I was returning home. I lived near London. It was winter and the weather was bad. I started my journey home early in the morning but I couldn't travel fast. The roads were covered with ice and I had to drive slowly and carefully. I was still a long way from home when it was dark. Then my car lamps began to fail. It was too dangerous to stay on the main road. The traffic was heavy there. I turned off into a quiet country road as soon as I could.

After a few miles I saw a road sign. *Millham* it said. Five minutes later I was driving along a narrow street with houses on both sides. It looked a friendly little place. There were a few shops with bright lights and I could see a garage at the end of the street. I pulled up there and explained my trouble to the garage man. He looked at my car lights. Then he looked at the engine. He shook his head. 'Your dynamo has broken. I'll repair it in the morning,' he said. 'But you can't drive any more tonight. It wouldn't be safe.'

'Is there a hotel in Millham?' I asked.

'Oh yes,' he answered, 'There's *The Goat* at the top of the street. You've just come past it. I think you'll get a bed there. We don't have many visitors in Millham in the winter. Tell Mr Richards that I'm mending your dynamo. He'll do his best for you.'

I thanked him, took my case out of the car, and walked

back up the street to *The Goat*. It was an old building and I could see through the window that there was a cheerful fire burning in the little dining room. The hotel office was just inside the front door and I rang the bell that stood on the desk.

A big man appeared through a door at the back of the office. He had a cloth in one hand and a half-full glass of beer in the other. He smiled at me in a friendly way.

'Mr Richards?' I asked.

He put his glass of beer down on the desk. 'Yes,' he answered. 'Can I help you?'

I explained that my car was at the garage. I said that I was in need of a meal and a room for the night.

'The meal is not a problem,' he said. 'Dinner will be ready in about an hour. The room is the difficulty. This is a small hotel, as you can see. We've only got six bedrooms and they are all taken. We are hardly ever full up in the winter. I'm sorry.'

I was just going to ask him what I could do, when the door opened again. A little woman walked quickly into the room.

'This is my wife,' Mr Richards explained. Then he turned to her and said, 'I was telling this gentleman that we are full tonight, Liz. His car is being repaired at the garage and he wants dinner and a bed for the night.'

'There's Room 7, Tom,' she said.

'But we don't——' He didn't finish his sentence. He picked up his glass of beer and drank it slowly while he listened to his wife.

'We can't turn the gentleman away on a night like this,' she said. 'I'll make up the bed in Room 7.'

'I'm giving you trouble, I'm afraid.'

'It's no trouble, Mr . . . ?'

'Saunders,' I said. 'I'm John Saunders.'

'It's no trouble, Mr Saunders. We don't use Room 7 much, that's all. You'll be comfortable there. There's nothing wrong with it.' She gave her husband a look when she said that, but he didn't reply to her.

'Come along, Mr Saunders,' he said, 'you can try a glass of our good beer. You won't find better beer in England than we keep at *The Goat*. Leave your case here in the office until your room is ready for you.'

He led the way to the bar, a warm cheerful room where people were drinking and chatting. I met some of the other visitors and some of the inhabitants of Millham who were having an evening drink in the bar. I felt happy and comfortable, especially when Mr Richards put a pint of his famous beer in front of me. He was right about it. It was a great drink. I was sorry when they told me that my room was ready!

I telephoned my wife from the hotel office and told her what had happened and where I was. I said that I'd be home the next day in time for lunch. Then I picked up my case and found Room 7. It was on the top floor, above the other bedrooms. It felt rather cold, but Mrs Richards had turned on the electric fire.

'It will soon warm up,' I thought, 'and it's beautifully quiet up here. I'll sleep well tonight.'

It wasn't a big room. There was space for the bed, a clothes cupboard, and a wash basin behind the door. Between the wash basin and the clothes cupboard there was a big straight-backed chair against the wall. That was all; but it was clean and I was pleased with it. I unpacked my case, washed, and then went down to dinner.

Mrs Richards was a good cook and I enjoyed my meal. I had a bottle of red wine with it. When I had finished my dinner, I returned to the bar. I chatted to Mr Richards and some of his friends until I began to feel sleepy.

'I think I'll go up to bed now,' I said. 'Can I have an early breakfast? I want to start my journey as soon as my car is ready.'

'Will eight o'clock be all right?'

'Oh, yes, thank you. I don't think that the dynamo will be repaired before nine.'

'Goodnight, then, Mr Saunders. I hope you'll be comfortable and sleep well.'

'I'm sure I shall, Mr Richards. Goodnight. Thank you for a very nice evening.'

The bedroom was warm and I turned off the electric fire. I lay in bed in great comfort and started to read, but my eyes were closing. I turned off the light and fell fast asleep.

I don't know how long I slept. But something woke me. I know that it wasn't a noise. The bedroom was quiet. But something strange was happening. The lamp on my bedside table was not turned on, but the room was slowly becoming light. At least, *part* of the room was becoming light. My bed was in the dark. I could not see the clothes cupboard or the washbasin, but I *could* see the big chair between them. I could see its seat, its arms, its legs and its tall straight back quite clearly. It was shining at me out of the dark.

I closed my eyes tightly. I didn't feel afraid. Not then. Fear came later. No, I wasn't afraid; but I wanted to think. I wanted to shut out that strange light and to explain things to myself. It couldn't be true that I had seen the chair. All the rest of the room was dark. I had been dreaming. Of course! I had drunk too much in the bar after dinner and I had been dreaming. I decided to count up to fifty very slowly. When I reached that number I was going to open my eyes. And the room would be dark. I *knew* it would be dark.

'. . . forty, forty-one . . .' I was counting the numbers very slowly indeed when I heard the noise. Somebody was breathing in the room. I lay very still and I listened. Oh, I listened very carefully! The sound of breathing continued . . . in . . . out . . . in . . . out . . . in . . . out . . . This was not a dream. A thief, perhaps?

I opened my eyes. I could still see the chair, but now

there was a man sitting in it. He was old and had white hair, but he sat up straight. His hands held the arms of the chair very tightly. His bright blue eyes were fixed on me.

I tried to speak, but no words came. I knew what I wanted to say: '*Who are you? What are you doing here? Get out of my room.*' I tried again, but it was no use. I lay there and waited. I told myself not to be afraid. He was too old to harm me. It was his stare that was so frightening. Those blue eyes of his never moved.

'He must do something soon,' I thought. 'He must say something.'

He seemed to hear my thoughts. He raised his left hand and pointed his finger at me. Now, I saw that his eyes were very sad. Suddenly, I had no fear of him. He was trying to tell me something. When he spoke, his voice was tired.

'I never found out,' he said, 'but you have.'

His hand dropped; and suddenly, I could speak. 'What have I found out?' I asked. 'Who are you? What——?' Before I could complete the question, he disappeared. Everything went dark.

A voice woke me. 'I've brought you a cup of tea, Mr Saunders. Your breakfast will be ready in half an hour.' Mr Richards put the tea on my bedside table and went out quickly, leaving me to my thoughts.

And I had plenty to think about. I had fallen asleep as soon as my strange visitor disappeared. Or had I really been asleep all the time? Had I dreamt the whole thing? Ought I to say anything about it to Mr and Mrs Richards? I decided that I ought not to speak to them about my strange visitor. They had been kind to me and had made me very comfortable. It wouldn't be fair to trouble them with a mystery that they couldn't solve. I couldn't blame them.

So I had my breakfast and went into the hotel office to pay my bill. Mrs Richards was sitting at the desk. I thanked her for looking after me so well. She smiled at me and gave me the bill. 'It's been a pleasure, Mr Saunders. We like to make our visitors comfortable at *The Goat*. Did you sleep well?'

I was counting out the money for the bill. When I looked up to answer her I saw a picture on the wall behind her. The white hair, the strong face and the bright blue eyes were terribly familiar to me.

I pointed at the picture. 'Who is that?' I asked.

She glanced at the picture and turned back quickly to me. 'It's Tom's father. He lived with us here at *The Goat*. He died five years ago. As a matter of fact, he died in the room you slept in last night. That's why Tom didn't want you to have Room 7.'

'But you——' I stopped. I had to choose my words carefully. I didn't know how much she knew. I didn't know how much she was willing to tell me. Before I could say anything, she was speaking again.

'There were some silly stories about Room 7, Mr Saunders. One or two nervous visitors said that they didn't sleep well in that room. They said they were afraid during the night, but they couldn't explain their fear. They said that the room was haunted. A ghost isn't good for a hotel, so Tom's father decided that he'd sleep in Room 7. He didn't believe that it was haunted. He said that he'd soon find out the cause of the trouble. He didn't believe in ghosts; and I don't, either. Well, he went up to bed at his usual time and in his usual state of good health, but. . .'

'Yes?' I said. 'And what happened? Go on.'

'I was fond of him,' she said, 'and it makes me sad to remember. I took tea up for him the next morning. I found him there—dead. He hadn't had time to undress and get into bed. He was sitting in that big chair, cold and dead. Of course, he was an old man. It could have happened at any time. The doctor said that it could. His heart had failed suddenly, the doctor said.'

She took the money and gave me my change. I put it in

my pocket and picked up my case.

'Mrs Richards,' I said, 'I think you ought to——'

She wasn't listening to me. She gave me a cheerful smile. Then she said: 'So, you see, Mr Saunders, we never did discover the mystery of Room 7. And I don't believe that anybody will. It's just a silly story.'

I said goodbye and I walked quickly down the street towards the garage.

The voice of an old man seemed to be following me: 'I never found out,' it said. 'I never found out whether Room 7 is haunted. But you have. You know now, don't you?'

The doctor's last visit

It was a warm summer's night in mid-July. The air was
still. A bright moon was high in the clear sky. The only
sound that young Police Constable Mitford could hear was
the sound of his own footsteps. Rayner Street was quiet.
There were no lights in any of its windows. Its inhabitants
were all in bed and fast asleep.

The young constable looked at his watch. It was half past
two in the morning. Suddenly, he felt very happy. He had
not been a policeman for very long and this was his first
patrol alone. Until tonight an older policeman had come on
duty with him. Now, P.C. Mitford had been sent out on
patrol alone. He had become a real policeman at last.

Half past two. At three o'clock he must return to the
police station to make his report. After that, he could go off
duty. Then he could go home. His first night as a real
policeman was ending.

He walked slowly on and watched the street carefully. He
had been trained to use his eyes. 'A good policeman
watches out all the time,' they had taught him. P.C. Mitford
wanted to be a good policeman, and his careful eyes missed
nothing that night. One of the downstairs windows in
Number 26 was open. Some garden tools had been left
outside the front door of Number 21.

'Careless people!' P.C. Mitford said to himself. 'They
think they are safe in a quiet street like this. They don't
think that thieves will cause trouble in Rayner Street.'

A large black cat ran across the road and jumped over the
garden wall of Number 13. Then it sat on the doorstep and
watched him go by. P.C. Mitford smiled.

'You've come home, have you?' he said. 'I shall soon be
going home, too. Goodnight, cat!'

He was feeling very cheerful. His night patrol was
ending.

When he was near the top of the street he saw a big white car parked outside Number 3. He made a note of its number—ZZB 777X. The doors of the car were all locked and it was parked correctly.

'Good,' he thought. 'At least one careful person lives in Rayner Street.'

He stood and looked at the front of Number 3. It was a big comfortable-looking place, but the garden was wild and the door was in need of paint.

'That's strange,' he thought. 'This isn't a poor man's house. Anyone who lives here can afford to look after his garden and paint his front door.'

P.C. Mitford moved on. He had walked a few yards past Number 3 when he heard a noise behind him. He turned round. The front door had opened. A man was running down the garden path towards the car. He was tall, he wore a dark suit, and he carried a case in his left hand. He looked white and ill. His eyes were wild and staring. They seemed too big for his face.

For a moment, he stood still by the big car. Then he turned away and ran down the street.

The constable ran after him. 'Stop!' he shouted. 'Stop! Who are you? Do you live here?'

The man did not answer. Mitford ran harder. He knew that he could catch him.

And then, at the end of Rayner Street, the man disappeared. One moment, he was there, a few yards ahead of the young policeman. The next moment, he had gone. The bright moon lit the whole street, and it was empty.

P.C. Mitford turned back towards Number 3. The car was still there. The garden was full of shadows—and the front door was open.

He knew what he must do. He must explore the house. Surely something very strange had happened at Number 3? But, suddenly, he was afraid. He didn't want to go through that open door. He took a deep breath. He walked up the

garden path. He had to do his duty.

The front door led into a big hall. He shone his powerful police torch round the hall. By its light he saw chairs and a table. They were covered in dust. He tried to turn on the electric lights, but nothing happened. The electricity had been cut off.

'Nobody lives here,' he thought. 'Nobody has lived here for a long time.'

And then he heard a noise. Somewhere in the house a woman was crying. He held his breath and listened. The noise rose and fell, but it did not stop. It was coming from an upstairs room.

He shone his torch round the hall again. He saw the stairs at the far end of the hall. Slowly, he moved towards them. He began to climb them. They were dusty—very dusty. His shoes were making clear marks in the dust. He looked back towards the hall. He shone his torch down at the hall floor. He could see the marks of his own feet. They were the only marks on that dusty floor.

P.C. Mitford's heart jumped. 'That man,' he thought, 'that man who ran out of this house a few minutes ago— why didn't his feet make marks on the hall floor? Why can I see only the marks of my own feet in the dust?'

He nearly turned back at that moment. 'After all,' he thought, 'I can keep watch on this house from outside. I can use my radio and call the police station. I can ask the Duty Officer for help. I can watch the house from the street until help comes. Sergeant Thomas will understand that I need help. I'll report to him what I have seen. I'll tell him about the strange man who ran away. I'll tell him that the front door of Number 3 was open. I'll tell him that I think there is somebody else still inside this house. I'll——'

But his chance to escape was lost. The woman's crying stopped. He heard a terrible scream from the bedroom at the top of the stairs.

'No! No! Please don't! Jonathan, please don't! Please!
...Please!...' And the scream died away in a terrible cry,
'*Aaah!*'

P.C. Mitford's training had been good. Sergeant Thomas
had taught him well. He had taught him that a policeman
must not run away from danger. Mitford knew what his
duty was. That terrible scream had been a cry for help.

He ran up the stairs. The bedroom door was locked. He
kicked hard at the lock...once...twice...three times. The
door sprang open.

He rushed in. The light of his torch travelled round the
room. He saw an empty chair—a dressing-table—an
overturned bedside table—a bed. On the bed lay a pile of
bedclothes. Mitford walked slowly towards the bed.
Perhaps somebody was hiding under that heavy pile of
bedclothes.

He moved his torch from his right hand into his left. He
kept the light pointing at the bed. Then he reached out and
pulled the clothes away from the bed.

A dead woman's face looked up at him. Her tongue was
sticking out of her open mouth. Her eyes shone in the
light of his torch. A terrible smell came from her yellow
skin.

'My God!' he said aloud. 'Murder on my first night
patrol. And I've let the murderer escape!'

He covered that terrible dead face with the bedclothes
and closed the bedroom door behind him. Outside
Number 3 he called the Duty Officer on his radio.

'P.C. Mitford, Sergeant. I'm outside Number 3, Rayner
Street. It's murder. I'm certain it's murder. And I've seen
the murderer and I've let him escape. He's about six feet
tall. He's about sixty years old. He's wearing a dark suit.
He's carrying a small case. The dead person is a woman,
about——'

Sergeant Thomas's familiar voice interrupted him.
'Report back to the police station immediately, Mitford.

Your patrol ends at three a.m. It's nearly three o'clock now.'

'But, Sergeant, there's a dead woman in this house and the murderer is escaping. I need——'

'Don't interrupt, Mitford. Just obey orders. Make sure that the door of Number 3 is locked. Then report back here at once. Your message has been received and understood.'

The radio went dead when Sergeant Thomas had finished. P.C. Mitford closed the door of Number 3. Then he tested it. It was safely locked.

It was a very troubled young policeman who walked slowly back to the police station.

'Sit down, Mitford. Drink this cup of tea.' Sergeant Thomas pushed a cup and saucer across the duty desk. 'Now,' he said, 'you can tell me what happened. Don't rush it. I shan't interrupt you.'

He listened quietly until the constable had finished his story.

'Right,' he said. 'Now answer some questions. First, what's the date?'

'It's July 13th, Sergeant. But what——?'

'Just answer my questions, Mitford. There's a lot you don't understand about tonight. There's a lot I don't understand, either. But I know a bit more about it than you do.'

'But that man, Sergeant. The man I saw running away in Rayner Street. We ought to have police cars out looking for him.'

'They wouldn't find him, Mitford. Nobody will find him.'

'But, Sergeant—'

'Just shut up, will you? This isn't an easy story to tell. It will be more difficult if you interrupt me.'

'Sorry, Sergeant.'

'Now, think hard. Where was the man when you heard the woman scream?'

'He. . .he was. . .he was somewhere in the street. He

must have been. That's where I last saw him. He wasn't in the house.'

'And the woman you think you saw, Mitford, how—?'

'Think, Sergeant! I don't *think* I saw her. I *did* see her.'

'All right, Mitford. Don't get excited. She was dead, you say?'

'She was dead.' Mitford's voice was very quiet. 'She looked...she looked...I was afraid of her, Sergeant...her tongue was...and that terrible smell...'

'Yes, yes. I know. You've described her already. And how long had she been dead?'

The young police constable did not answer. He covered his face with his hands.

'Come on, Mitford. You must have some idea. Had she just died when you saw her? Had the man you saw in the street just killed her?'

'No, Sergeant.' Mitford sat up straight in his chair again. 'No, she hadn't just died. And he hadn't killed her just before I saw her.'

'How do you know?'

'Because...because he wasn't in the house when I heard her crying and screaming. And because—oh, my God!—because she'd been dead for years. That thing I saw was—'

'All right, Mitford. All right. It's been a bad night for you, but you've got to hear the rest. The man that you thought you saw in Rayner Street has also been dead for years. No, don't interrupt. I can't *explain* anything. I can only give you the facts. You are not the first policeman to report this story. It's all happened before on this date. Does that make you feel better?'

Mitford nodded. 'At least I know I'm not going crazy, Sergeant. If other policemen have seen the same thing—'

'They have. Now, listen. A doctor—Dr Jonathan Tennyson—and his wife used to live at Number 3, Rayner Street. He was a good doctor. Everybody liked him. His wife was a terrible woman. She drank too much. When she was drunk she often attacked him. Once, she tried to set fire to the house. One night—or, I should say, early one morning—he came home after visiting a sick man. She was drunk. She was crying and shouting and screaming. He was tired and nervous. He became angry and violent. He was not a violent man, Mitford, but this time he became very violent. He broke her neck with his hands as she lay screaming in her bed. Then he ran out of the house.'

They were both silent for a time.

'What happened to him, Sergeant?' Mitford's quiet question broke the silence.

'He ran like a wild thing until he reached the London road. He tried to cross it. He ran straight into the traffic. A heavy lorry killed him.'

Mitford was silent again.

'When did all this happen, Sergeant?' he asked at last.

'Ten years ago. In the early morning of July 13th.'

'What about the big white car? How does that come into the story?'

'It doesn't. It belongs to the man who lives in Number 22. He parks it outside Number 3. The street is wider there. And nobody has lived in Number 3 since the doctor and his wife died.'

Sergeant Thomas was silent again. Then he said, 'You'd better write your report in the duty book, Mitford. Then go home. You look tired.'

Mitford picked up the pen. 'Shall I report what I saw at Number 3, Sergeant?'

'No,' said Sergeant Thomas. 'Better not.'

Mrs Wood comes home

I always used to go to Porchester for my holidays. It is a
quiet little town, full of old and interesting buildings. Very
few visitors ever go there, so there are no crowds. I enjoyed
its sleepy atmosphere. I work in a big city, so a holiday in
Porchester was a complete change from my usual life.
Besides, I was studying the history of the place. I wanted to
learn about its past life, the story of its people and its
buildings. I made notes about all these things during my
holidays and I soon knew more about the history of
Porchester than most of the people who lived there.

I am not a rich man and I cannot afford to stay in hotels.
When Jack Thompson heard that I wanted to spend my
holidays in Porchester he invited me to stay with him. He
and I were in the Army together during the war and we
were good friends. So I stayed with him and his wife,
Annie, in their pretty little house in Fore Street. I paid
them some money, of course. I am not the kind of man to
let my friends pay for me. But they always said that they
looked forward to my visits. They used to tell me that my
holidays were a holiday for them. I'm sure they meant it.
We had some very happy times together...until...until
Mrs Wood came home.

That year, I went there as usual for Easter. It was a fine
spring afternoon when I arrived. Little white clouds, a blue
sky and an hour or two of warm sunshine. We went for a
walk and I took photographs of the church.

'You must have hundreds of photographs of Porchester,'
Annie said.

'I *have* got a lot,' I answered, 'but I need them. A
student of history must use his eyes. When I am away from
Porchester I look at my photographs. They help me to
understand the story of the past.'

We had a drink at *The Rose and Crown*, a nice little public house. Then we walked home to Fore Street and after supper we sat talking by the fireside.

'Tell me all the news,' I said. 'I haven't been in Porchester since last summer. I want to know about everything.'

Jack smiled. 'You don't really think that Porchester has changed, Bill? You know us better than that. Life moves very slowly here. We've got a new doctor, if that interests you. Old Dr Mitchell went away in October. He's gone to live with his sister in the country. Young Dr Warren has come in place of him. He seems very nice.'

'Everything about Porchester interests me,' I answered. 'Go on telling me the news.'

'Mrs Wood has gone away,' Annie said.

'Mrs Wood?' I asked. 'Who is she? Where did she live? I don't think I know her.'

'I don't think you do know her,' Annie answered. 'She never went out very much when she lived here.'

'Where did you say she lived?'

'I didn't say.' Annie smiled at me. 'Wait a minute, Bill, and I'll tell you as much as I know. Mrs Wood is a very old woman. She didn't go out very much because she can't walk very well. Just before Christmas she went away. She is staying with her son in Australia. She lived in the house across the street. The one with the big bush in front of the windows.'

'I know,' I said. 'I often used to think that somebody was looking out of the upstairs window. I couldn't be sure because the bush covers part of the window.'

'Mrs Wood spent most of her time staring out of that window.' Jack spoke angrily. He was such a kind man that I was surprised. I had never seen him angry before.

'Be fair, Jack,' Annie said. 'She was lonely. Of course she liked to watch people. She didn't feel so lonely when she could sit at her window and see what was happening outside.'

'If she was lonely it was her own fault. Don't you remember how rude she was to you?'

'We agreed that we wouldn't talk about that again,' said Annie. 'And you can't blame the old woman because she sat at her window. Watching people in the street gave her pleasure. I was sorry for her.'

'I'm sorry for her son,' Jack answered. 'I wouldn't like to have that old woman living in my house. But I hope they don't quarrel too much. I hope she stays with him for ever. She won't be lonely there. I don't want her back here in Fore Street.'

'Jack! You are—'

I don't know what Annie was going to say. I could see that they were both becoming angry. I changed the conversation by asking about the new doctor. We didn't talk about Mrs Wood any more, and my two friends were soon happy again. They were usually gentle with each other, and I was surprised that an old woman could trouble them.

I went to bed quite early, but I couldn't go to sleep. I looked at my watch. It was midnight. I tried to read a book, but it did not hold my interest. I was thinking about Jack and Annie. Why were they so troubled by Mrs Wood? That lonely old woman was far away in Australia, but they became angry about her. Annie tried to be fair, but she didn't like her. She was sorry for her. At least, she *said* she was sorry for her. But I thought that Annie was just as angry about Mrs Wood as Jack was. The difference was that Annie wouldn't let her angry thoughts show.

I got out of bed and went to the window. I stared across the street at Mrs Wood's house. The moon was shining brightly and I could see the front of the house clearly. The leaves of the big bush moved slowly in the gentle wind.

'What a lovely night!' I said to myself. 'The weather is

going to be fine for my holiday.'

I noticed that there were curtains at Mrs Wood's windows. She had not left the house empty. It looked like a house that was still lived in. The curtains at the windows made me think that the house had an inhabitant. 'Perhaps you are still there, Mrs Wood,' I thought.

Then I saw the curtain at one of the upstairs windows move. Somebody was sitting there! Mrs Wood was trying to see me clearly!

I was filled with fear. I turned away from the window and jumped into bed. I lay there in the dark. I felt terrible. She had been watching me. I knew she had.

Slowly, I got my courage back. 'You fool!' I said to myself. 'That curtain didn't move. The leaves of the bush are moving when the wind blows. That was what you saw. The wind blew the leaves across the window, and you thought that the curtain moved. Besides, she can't hurt you. If Mrs Wood *is* in her house, she can't hurt you. She's a lonely old woman. You are a strong, healthy man. What are you afraid of? And, anyway, she is *not* in her house. She is in Australia. She is staying with her son.'

I felt better then, but it was a long time before I went to sleep. When I did sleep I had bad dreams. In my dreams I was trying to escape from a strange dark house—and an old woman was watching me.

I felt tired and unhappy when I woke. My holiday was starting badly. I washed and dressed. Then I opened my bedroom window and took a photograph of Mrs Wood's house. The morning sun was throwing light across the front of the house. The bush was throwing a shadow. The house looked very pretty and I was careful with the photograph. I wanted to get a really good picture.

Then I put my camera away and went downstairs. Jack was alone in the kitchen.

'What's the matter?' he asked. 'You look tired.'

'I didn't sleep very well.'

'Nor did Annie,' he said, 'so I've made her stay in bed.
She had bad dreams. She was dreaming about that old
woman who lived across the road, I think.'

We didn't talk much while we ate. When we'd finished
breakfast I questioned him.

'Jack,' I said, 'tell me about Mrs Wood. Why did you get
angry last night when you and Annie were talking about
her?'

'That was silly of me,' he answered. 'I shouldn't let her
make me angry. After all, she's not here now. She is far
away. She's in Australia.'

'You haven't answered me,' I said. 'She's an old woman.
She *is* far away, but you and Annie quarrel about her. Why?'

'I'll tell you. Annie tried to help her. She often went to
see her. She went shopping for her. She often cooked for
her. She sat and talked to her. I *should* say she often sat and
listened to her. The old woman would rather talk than
listen.'

'You didn't go across there with Annie?'

'No. I never liked Mrs Wood. I never wanted Annie to
spend so much time with her. And I was right. In the end,
she behaved very badly to Annie.'

Jack stopped speaking. I waited for him to continue, but
he was staring at the kitchen window. He wasn't looking at
me. He had forgotten I was there.

'Jack,' I said, 'I'm waiting. Tell me the rest of your
story.'

He turned towards me. 'One day,' he said, 'Annie came
back from seeing Mrs Wood. She looked tired and ill. I
asked her what was the matter. She didn't want to tell me,
but I made her. She said that Mrs Wood had been rude and
angry. She had made Annie afraid of her...Annie never
went there again...she could not forget what Mrs Wood
had said...'

Jack's story wasn't very clear, but I listened carefully and
I understood the sense of it. The old woman knew

30

that Jack didn't like her. She told Annie that she hated him. Annie tried to make excuses for Jack. She told Mrs Wood that she didn't understand him. He was a kind and a good man, she said—but the old woman wouldn't listen to her. She shouted at Annie. She told her that she was as bad as her husband. She told her that she would drive them both out of their house.

I waited until Jack had finished speaking. Then I said, 'That's a very nasty story. Mrs Wood is a terrible old woman, but I don't understand why you and Annie let her trouble you. She's gone away. She can't hurt you. If she were here she couldn't hurt you. She's a silly, angry old woman.'

Jack looked at me. 'Why didn't *you* sleep last night?' he asked.

I didn't enjoy my holiday. I went for long walks. I took photographs. I studied the history of Porchester. I did all the things that I always did, but I did not enjoy them.

Jack and Annie were kind to me. We were as fond of each other as we always had been, but there was something wrong. They were in trouble. They quarrelled. At night they did not sit talking by the fireside. They stood and stared through their front window. They stood and stared at Mrs Wood's house. And each night when I went to bed I thought I saw her face at her window. I wanted to get back home. I was glad when my holiday ended and I could escape from Porchester. I couldn't help Jack and Annie. I tried to help them, but they wouldn't listen to me.

After I had been at home for a few days the postman delivered my holiday photographs. I had posted the films before I left Porchester and now they were ready for me to see. Usually, I rushed to look at my photographs. I could hardly wait to see them; but now, I was afraid. I stood and stared at the packet. I didn't dare to open it. I was afraid of what I was going to see.

At last, I found my courage and I made myself undo the packet. Slowly, I searched through the photographs until I found the one that I feared to see. There it was—the photograph that I had taken so carefully—the photograph of Mrs Wood's house. I felt sick. Everything was clear and bright—the garden, the bush, the front door. And, at an upstairs window, an old woman's face was staring through the glass!

I was still holding that terrible photograph when the door of my flat flew open. Jack rushed into the room. He looked wild—so wild and strange that I hardly recognized him. I tried to hide the photograph but I was too late. He tore it out of my hand.

'There she is,' he said. 'That thing looking through the window is Mrs Wood.'

'But, Jack, it can't be. . . she's far away. . . she's . . .'

He didn't let me finish. I shall never forget his words or the terrible look on his face as he spoke.

'Bill,' he said, 'Mrs Wood died in Australia on the day that you came to Porchester to begin your holiday. We heard the news soon after you left.'

'Then. . . what?. . . how do you explain?' I pointed to the face at the window.

'I don't,' he said. 'I can't. All I know is—she came home.'

A new fear swept over me. 'Annie!' I shouted. 'Jack, how is Annie? Does she know that Mrs Wood came home?'

He looked old and ill. I thought that he was going to fall down. I put my hand on his arm and guided him to a chair. At last he spoke. His voice was so weak that I could hardly hear him.

'Last night,' he said, 'there was a knock at our door. Annie went to open it. I was in the kitchen, but I could hear her voice. She called out. It was a great cry of fear that I shall never forget. *"Mrs Wood,"* she said, *"you've come home!"* I ran to the door. Annie lay there—dead. The doctor said that fear killed her.'

The ghost in the garden

I had worked hard all my life. When I was sixty years old
I decided to stop working. I sold my house in the city and
I bought a house in the country. I had always wanted to
live in the country. I wanted the quietness of country life
after the noise and rush of the city. I wanted a big garden
where I could grow flowers and vegetables. My wife agreed
with my ideas. She was born in the country and she wanted
to get back to a quiet life. She shared my love of gardening.
One day I told her that I had saved enough money to give
up work. She was very pleased.

'Henry,' she said, 'I have been looking forward to this for
years. We have always shared the same interests. Now, we
shall have time to enjoy them together.'

So we started to look for a house in the country. It
wasn't easy to find the kind of house we wanted. We did not
want a big house, but we wanted a big garden. It had to be
a sunny house, too. We travelled miles to look at houses for
sale. Each time we saw a 'For Sale' board outside a house
we stopped to have a look at the building. None of them
pleased us. The search went on for months and we became
very tired. If we had not shared the same ideas about
houses we might have quarrelled. But we knew what we
wanted and we were sure that we would find it.

'We must go on trying,' we said to each other. 'The next
house for sale may be the one we are looking for.'

At last, we found the house we had been dreaming of. In
a village in Hampshire, about fifty miles from London, we
discovered *Samways*. It was just the right size for us. It
was built of stone. It was warm, sunny and comfortable.
Between the front of the house and the quiet village street
was a little garden. A path led up to the front door steps. At
the back there was a big garden full of fruit trees and
flowers. The sun was shining and the back garden was filled

with light and warmth.

When we saw the 'For Sale' board outside *Samways* we looked at each other and said, 'This house is for us. We must buy it.'

We didn't argue about the price. It seemed cheap to us. We wanted *Samways*. If the price had seemed dear, we wouldn't have argued about it. Our long search had ended. We paid the money and bought the house of our dreams.

We moved into *Samways* in the late spring. There was a lot to do. There always is a lot to do when you move from one house to another. We had been living in a modern flat in the city. *Samways* was an old house. We bought tables, chairs, cupboards and beds that looked right in *Samways*. We had to get carpets, too, and curtains for the windows. We took care to see that everything fitted properly and looked nice. This was going to be our home for the rest of our lives.

And we worked hard in the garden through the spring and summer of that year. The weather was dry and warm, so we worked outside every day. Often, we did not stop until it was dark. The house had been empty for several years, so the garden was wild. We dug the flower and vegetable beds. We cut back the wild trees and bushes. We sowed seeds and we planted new flowers. By the end of August we were sure that our garden was going to be as beautiful as our house.

At tea time one day in September I was working alone in the garden. My wife had gone into the house to get our tea ready. I heard her calling to me through the open window of the sitting room.

'Henry,' she called. 'Tea is ready and we've got a visitor. Mr Barnes has come to see us. He's going to have tea with us.'

Mr Barnes was the village priest. We had seen him when we went to church, of course, but he had not visited us before.

'I'm glad you've come,' I said. 'Joan and I are very pleased to see you at *Samways*.'

'It's a beautiful old house,' the priest answered. 'Everybody in the village is pleased that you have come to live here. You are making a wonderful difference to the house and garden, Mr Chapman.'

'Thank you,' I said. 'When we've had tea you must have a look at the big garden. You've seen only the little one at the front.'

'I'd like to do that,' he answered. 'I'm very interested in gardens, but I don't get much time to work in mine.'

'You must be busy,' Joan said. 'Do you visit most people in the village?'

'I try to visit them all. I think the village priest should know everybody who lives in the village. It's an important part of his job. I haven't been to see you and Mr Chapman before today because I knew how busy *you* were. But I have noticed you both in church.'

While we had tea we chatted about the village and its history. Mr Barnes knew a great deal about the old village families. He told us interesting stories about the past. He knew about the history of the church and the houses and farms of the village. Both Joan and I liked him. He was friendly and he loved the village and its inhabitants. He seemed to be a good, kind man and a good priest.

When we had finished tea we went into the garden. Mr Barnes knew quite a lot about gardens as well as about history. He talked very sensibly about the changes we had made. That pleased us. Gardeners enjoy talking about their gardens. He also seemed to like the work we had done. That pleased us even more. We decided that we liked the village priest very much indeed.

Then he said that he must be going, so we walked back towards the house.

'Tell me,' said Mr Barnes, 'do you know how your house got its rather strange name?'

'No,' said Joan, 'we don't. I've been wondering whether you knew.'

'It was built by a man whose name was Samways,' Mr Barnes said. 'In the country a house is often given the name of its builder. Your house was built by Elijah Samways about three hundred years ago. He built it for himself—he was a wealthy man—and he was the first person to live here.'

'Did he have a family?' I asked.

'No. He lived here alone, without wife or children. He just had one old servant—a man—to look after him.'

'And what happened when Elijah Samways died?' Joan asked.

'His house was sold. Nobody with his name has lived here since he died. But you have now bought his house and its name is still *Samways*. I think that's rather nice, don't you?'

We did, and we said so. Then I remembered something else.

'Mr Barnes,' I said, 'there's one more big job to do in the garden. Look at this tree.'

I pointed at a big ash tree near the wall of the house. It was as tall as the house itself. Its branches were nearly touching our bedroom window.

'It will have to be cut down,' I said. 'It's too near the house. It will be dangerous when the winter winds begin to blow.'

Before Mr Barnes could reply, Joan spoke. 'Oh, no, Henry. We've talked about this before.'

She turned to the priest. 'Tell him that he's wrong, Mr Barnes. It's a beautiful tree. It's strong and healthy. It would be a great shame to cut it down.'

The priest looked at the tree for a long time. He seemed to be wondering what to say. At last, he spoke to me very slowly.

'I must say that I agree with Mrs Chapman. It *is* a

36

beautiful tree. I do not think that it is dangerous. You can cut those top branches back if you think they are too long. But if you take my advice you will leave the tree alone. It was growing here before Elijah Samways built the house.'

'Well, well,' I said, 'we won't do anything in a hurry. We'll wait until winter comes before we decide.'

Winter came late that year. The long hot summer was followed by a warm dry autumn. Our work in the garden was a great happiness to us both. I did not think about the ash tree while the fine days lasted.

Then, in early November, the winds began to blow and the rain came. Winter was with us. We sat in our comfortable sitting room during the daytime. We read books and listened to our records and radio. At night, we had our evening meal and went to bed early. Sometimes during the day I used to put on my raincoat and go into the garden. I couldn't do any work there, but I watched the ash tree. When the wind blew hard its branches rose and fell. They looked like arms when they moved in the air, high above my head. They seemed to be sending a message to me, but I could not read their signs. Sometimes I used to stand out there for a long time and stare at the tree. I was trying to solve its mystery. One day, when I had been standing there longer than usual, Joan called to me from the house.

'Henry! What *are* you doing out there in the rain? You'll be wet through.'

'I'm coming, dear,' I answered.

But before I returned to the house I got my big saw and I climbed up the tree. I cut back the two branches that were close to our bedroom window. Mr Barnes was quite right, I thought. The ash tree was strong and healthy. There was no need to cut it down. But I felt safer when those branches were shorter.

I told Joan what I had done. She smiled at me. 'I'm so

glad that you agree, Henry,' she said. 'The tree is not dangerous. Now, take off your wet coat and have a cup of coffee.'

And that is what I did. We sat comfortably in front of the sitting room fire. We were both happy because we agreed with each other. The problem of the ash tree had been solved.

At the end of November the winter storms grew worse. Each day the wind blew stronger. When the wind stopped, the rain fell heavily. Then the wind started again. We lay in bed at night and listened to the storms. We fell asleep at last with the sound of the wind in our ears. And while we were sleeping it blew through our dreams.

On November 30th—I cannot forget *that* date—I woke up in the middle of the night. The lamp on Joan's bedside table was lit. She was sitting up in bed.

'What's the matter?' I asked. 'Can't you sleep?'

'Sh!. . . Sh!. . . . Listen!'

I lay still and listened. I heard the sound of the wind and nothing else.

'What's the matter?' I asked her again. 'What are you afraid of?'

'There's a noise. I can't hear it now, but it woke me up. Somebody has been knocking at the window.'

'Joan, dear,' I said, 'don't be silly! You've been dreaming. Lie down and go to sleep. There's nothing to be afraid of.'

'I'm not being silly, Henry. I heard it plainly. Somebody or something is knocking at that window. Louder than the noise of the wind.'

I got out of bed. 'I'll go down to the kitchen and make you a hot drink. You are too nervous to sleep. Some hot milk will make you feel better.'

Before I could open the bedroom door she called to me. Her voice was full of fear.

'I'm coming with you, Henry. Don't leave me here alone.

Not——'

She did not finish her sentence. Her face was white. She pointed at the window.

And this time I heard it, too.

Knock...knock...knock.

There, at the bedroom window. Slow, heavy knocks. Loud enough to be heard above the sound of the wind.

Knock...knock...knock.

I moved towards the window. Then I stopped. The knocks were repeated—louder. I was afraid. I was afraid to pull back the curtains. I was afraid to look through the window. I was afraid of seeing something terrible.

While I stood there, Joan spoke again. 'It's all right, Henry,' she said. 'I know what it is. Those long branches are knocking against the window. The wind is blowing hard and the branches are moving up and down.'

She had forgotten that I had cut the branches short. They were now too short to reach the window. I knew that the branches were not the cause of that terrible sound.

Before I could remind her of that fact she pulled back the curtains. Then she screamed; and my heart seemed to stop.

A face was looking through the window. It was the face of an old man. His long white hair was blowing in the wind. His head was close to the glass. His hands were raised. He began to beat them against the window...knock...knock ...knock.

I took a step forward. 'For God's sake!' I cried. 'Shut him out!'

I pulled the curtains across the window and I turned towards Joan. She was sitting on the bed. Her face was hidden in her hands. I put my arm round her.

'Come along,' I said, 'we'll go down to the kitchen. We can't stay in this room—not with that face at the window.'

She put her hand in mine and I led her to the door.

'His eyes, Henry!' she said. 'Did you notice his eyes? They were sad...terribly sad eyes, Henry. It is a sad ghost

that we have seen.'

Daylight returned at last. The wind dropped. The morning was cold and bright. At nine o'clock I telephoned Mr Barnes. He came at once and drank coffee with us while he listened to our story. When we had finished, he asked some questions.

'An old man's face, you say?'

I nodded.

'With long white hair?'

'Yes.'

'Did he seem angry? Did he want to make you afraid?'

'Oh no!' Joan answered the question before I could speak. 'No, Mr Barnes, I'm sure he wasn't angry. He made us afraid, but he didn't want to. His face was very sad. He seemed to be asking for help. I'm ashamed because we didn't help him, but we *were* afraid.'

'Don't blame yourself,' answered the priest. He spoke to my wife very gently. 'Of course you were afraid. Anybody would have been afraid. But I think that you may be able to help him.'

'How?' I asked. 'You seem to know something about the man. You'd better tell us, hadn't you? If this terrible thing happens here we shall not be able to live in this house.'

'I think I can solve the mystery,' he said. 'I told you that Elijah Samways lived here with one old servant. I didn't tell you the rest of the story, but I must tell you now. One night, thieves killed Elijah Samways and stole all his money. The thieves were never caught, but the old servant, Robert Forester, was accused of helping them. He said that he was innocent. He had been asleep all night, he said, and he had heard nothing. But he was accused of letting the thieves into the house. He was a poor old man with no family and no friends. Nobody believed that he was innocent. It was terrible...terrible...a terrible thing was done.'

'Go on, please,' Joan said, quietly. 'Tell us everything.'

'Yes,' he said, 'I must; but it's a fearful story. Robert Forester was killed in the garden at *Samways*. He said again and again that he was innocent, but they hanged him from a branch of the big ash tree. The thieves escaped, but an innocent man was hanged.'

'You believe that he was innocent?' I asked.

'I do now. I believe that he was falsely accused. I believe that he was trying to tell you that he was innocent. He appeared to you last night to beg for help.'

'Why did it happen last night?'

'It was November 30th. Robert Forester was hanged on that date, three hundred years ago.'

'How can we help him?' asked Joan.

'We must show him that we believe him. We must tell him that we know he was innocent.'

'But how?'

'Follow me.'

Mr Barnes led us into the garden to the ash tree.

'Robert Forester was buried here,' he said. 'This is his grave.'

'Here? But this is not a churchyard.'

'No. It is not holy ground. They did not believe that he was innocent. They would not allow him to be buried in the churchyard. They buried him near this tree. They buried him where they hanged him. But we will make this holy ground. It shall become a quiet grave. We will pray for Robert Forester.'

The priest knelt down on the cold, wet ground. Joan and I followed his example. He prayed for Robert Forester, and we joined in the prayers. He prayed for that innocent man. He prayed that his enemies should be forgiven. Then he took off the cross that he wore round his neck. He planted it firmly in the ground. The grave had been made holy.

'He will rest now,' said the priest, and we went back into the quiet house.

Roger Wingate's new car

'How much?' he asked.

The answer surprised and pleased him. It wasn't cheap, but you don't hope to buy a big, powerful car cheaply. The price was lower than he had thought it would be.

'It's only a year old, you say?'

'That's right. One year old. We know the man who owned it. We sold it to him. Now we are selling it for him. He's decided to stop driving. We've looked after it since it was new. It's a good car. At this price it's a very good car indeed.'

Roger thought hard. The garage man was right. It was a good car. The price was good and Roger could afford it.

'I'll buy it,' he said. 'I'll come for it tomorrow evening when I leave the office.'

And so, the next evening, he sat behind the wheel of his big new car. He drove carefully through the city traffic. Soon, he was leaving the busy streets behind. When he reached the quieter roads he drove faster. The powerful engine made driving a pleasure. The big headlamps lit the dark road far ahead of him. Roger Wingate was very pleased with his new car. It was worth a lot more than he had paid for it.

At the crossroads he had to stop. The traffic lights were red. He lit a cigarette and listened happily to the music on the car radio.

Suddenly, his heart jumped. A voice spoke very quietly. It was—or it seemed to be—a woman's voice.

'Turn right here,' it said.

For a moment, Roger thought that the voice had come from the radio. He was alone in the car. But the radio was still playing music. And when the voice spoke again he *knew* that it did not come from the radio. It spoke into his ear. It seemed to come from the passenger seat by his side.

'Turn right here,' it said again.

It was the voice of a young woman: a clear, light voice. It spoke so clearly that he turned to look at the seat. Somebody *must* be sitting there. But the seat was empty, of course. There was nothing to be afraid of, but Roger Wingate was afraid.

Another sound broke through his troubled thoughts. There were other cars behind him. Their drivers were angry. They were blowing their horns and making a terrible noise with their engines. Roger glanced at the traffic lights. They had changed to green. He was in the way of all the cars behind him and their drivers were signalling him to move on. He drove off slowly and they passed him one by one. Each driver blew his horn at him as he went by.

But Roger was not thinking about the angry drivers and their noisy horns. The sound of that quiet voice was still in his ears. *Turn right here.* He began to wonder about the road that went off to the right. It seemed to lead into a quiet street, but he had never been into it. The way to his house was straight ahead, so he had never turned right at the crossroads.

His wife was very pleased with the new car. She thought it was much more comfortable than their old one. She looked forward to a trip in it at the weekend. 'We'll take my mother with us,' she said. 'We'll go to the seaside and have a picnic. That will be fun, won't it, Roger?'

He didn't answer. He was staring at the new car through their sitting room window.

'Won't it be fun?' she asked again.

'Eh? Oh...er...yes, of course. Yes...I shall enjoy that.'

'I can't understand you, Roger. What's the matter with you? You've just bought this lovely car and you don't seem at all pleased. You are hardly listening to a word that I say.'

'I'm sorry, dear,' he said. 'As a matter of fact, I've got a rather difficult job at the office and I was thinking of that.

I'll have to go to work early in the morning so I'll go to bed soon. I'm in need of a good night's sleep.'

But he didn't tell her about the voice he had heard in the new car.

On his way to the office he went to see his old friend Bill Harper. Bill worked on a newspaper and he wasn't easily surprised by anything. He listened to Roger's story quietly. Then he asked him a question.

'You don't know the street to the right of the crossroads?'

'No.'

'It's a quiet, narrow little street. There are a few trees on each side and some nice houses. It's called Monmouth Road.'

'You've been there, Bill?'

'Once,' answered Bill. 'About a year ago.'

'You do believe me? You believe that I heard that voice?'

'I'm sure that *you* believe that you heard it. That's the important thing.'

Bill went to a cupboard and took out a small tape recorder. He passed it over to Roger.

'Here,' he said, 'carry that in your car on your way home tonight. Switch it on just before you reach the crossroads. Switch it off when you have passed the traffic lights. Bring it back to me tomorrow morning and we'll listen to the tape together. Promise not to play the tape before you bring it back.'

Roger nodded. 'I'll do what you say. I need help, Bill. That voice was real to me. I heard it and it seemed to have a message for me. I don't know what the message was but...'

Bill smiled at him. 'It's all right, Roger. I know you are troubled by this. I believe your story and I'll help you if I can. We're old friends, remember. Use that tape recorder on the way home and bring it back tomorrow.'

The next morning Roger put the tape recorder down on Bill's desk. His face was white.

'Yes,' he said. 'Yes. You needn't ask me. I heard it. Just like last night. But did this thing hear it?' —he pointed at the tape recorder as he spoke—'If it didn't, you won't believe me. You'll think I'm making it up.'

'Gently, Roger, gently!' Bill made him sit down. 'You're in too much of a hurry. Let's listen to the tape. We don't know yet what's on it. When we've heard it we can begin to explore your mystery.'

He opened the recorder and wound the tape back to the beginning.

Roger sat uncomfortably on the edge of his chair. He lit a cigarette nervously.

'I didn't use the car radio last night,' he said. 'I didn't want too much noise on the tape.'

'Good! I forgot to tell you not to switch on the radio. I'm glad you thought of that.'

Bill switched on. The tape began to run. At first, they heard only the noise of the engine. Then they could hear the sound of the tyres on the road.

'I opened the car window,' Roger explained. 'I needed fresh air.'

'Sh! Be quiet! I knew what you'd done.'

Then the noise of the engine fell. It was running very quietly.

'I was slowing down. The traffic lights were red. I knew that I must stop.'

'Shut up, Roger! I'm not a fool, you know. I understand what's happening.'

Roger closed his eyes and sat back in his chair. His heart beat quickly. He was nervous—no, he was afraid! He was afraid that the voice would not speak. Perhaps the tape recorder had not worked. Perhaps something had gone wrong. Bill would not believe him. He would not believe that he had heard that voice. And then he wouldn't be able to help him. Every evening Roger would have to start his journey home, and he would be afraid—afraid of the moment when the voice would speak. And one evening, when the voice had spoken, he would obey the command. Instead of driving straight on, he would turn right. He would obey that voice. He knew *now* that the command could not be refused. Instead of going home, he would turn right. He would obey the voice and drive his car into the mystery and danger waiting for him in Monmouth Road.

'Oh, God!' he said to himself, 'Make the voice speak *now*, on the tape. Make Bill believe me. Make him help me . . . *please* . . . I am afraid . . .'

On the tape the noise of the engine died down. The car had stopped at the traffic lights. For a second there was hardly a sound to be heard.

Then, in that clear light voice, came that familiar and terrible command: *Turn right here . . .*

Roger's breath escaped in a great shout. 'You heard it, Bill! You believe me! You *must* believe me now!'

Bill switched off the tape recorder. He turned to Roger and spoke very quietly. 'I heard it. I believe you, Roger. She's young. I thought she would be.'

'What do you mean?'

'Not now, Roger. I'll explain later. When you've finished at the office come round here and pick me up. I'm going to travel back with you tonight!'

The car left the busy streets behind. In the quieter roads Roger drove faster. Bill sat beside him. Neither man spoke. They were nervous . . . waiting . . .

They saw the traffic lights ahead. A green light shone towards them.

'What shall I do if the light stays green? It's turned red for the past two nights and I've had to stop at the crossroads.'

'It won't make any difference. She'll speak to you sooner if the light stays green.'

'How do you know?'

'Sh! Don't talk. Just listen and obey.'

They were nearly at the crossroads and the light was still green. Roger's mouth was dry and his heart hammered. He glanced at his friend. Bill was staring ahead and he was watching the green light.

Turn right here—it was the same voice, but clearer and stronger. She knew that her command would be obeyed.

'Now!' said Bill. 'Into Monmouth Road. And watch! Watch out for trouble!'

Roger turned the wheel. The big car rolled into the quiet little road. A few street lamps made small lakes of light in the darkness. The trees threw deep shadows across the front of the houses and on the road.

In the darkness under one of the trees a girl was standing. She moved forward. The headlamps of the car lit her up. They could see her clearly. She shone against the blackness of the night. She was young—twenty—twenty-five, perhaps. Beautiful—dressed for a party or a dance.

Bill took a deep breath. 'This is it!' he said. 'Be very careful, Roger. Look out!'

The girl threw herself into the road in front of the car. The wheel kicked in Roger's hands as he pulled it hard round. The tyres screamed. The heavy vehicle hit the tree hard, then came to rest.

Roger jumped out of the car. He shouted in a crazy voice: 'My God, I've run over her! I've killed her! Bill! Bill, where are you? Help!'

Bill was by his side. His voice was quiet. 'It's all right, Roger. Don't be afraid. You haven't hurt her. Look! The road is empty. Quiet, now. Be quiet. It's all right, I tell you.'

'But...where?...where's she gone? I saw her...she was standing there...surely you saw her too?...then she...'

48

'Yes, I saw her. And I saw what she did. But she's not here now. She's far away, Bill. Quiet, now! I'll get a taxi and take you home. The garage will fetch your car. You can't drive it.'

'I feel better now,' Roger put down his empty coffee cup. 'Please tell us what you know, Bill.'

'Yes, Bill, please explain,' Roger's wife said. 'It's been a terrible night. You and Roger had a narrow escape.'

'We did.' Bill spoke very slowly. 'Yes, we could be dead now. I think she wanted to kill somebody. But I'm not sure that she wanted to kill us. I'm not *sure* of anything.'

'Go on. Please go on.'

'I'll try, but it's very difficult. This is a story that I shall never write. It's a story that nobody would believe. I told you, Roger, that I'd been in Monmouth Road once, didn't I?'

'Yes. But you didn't tell me why you had been there.'

'I didn't think it was sensible to tell you, then. Now, I *must* tell you.'

He took his pipe out of his pocket and lit it carefully. He was thinking hard.

'I recognized that girl,' he said, at last.

'You did? How? Who is she?'

'Wait, please! Listen. Her name is . . .' Bill stopped speaking. Then he started again. 'I should say, her name *was* Kathleen Henson. She was killed in Monmouth Road. But she wasn't killed by you, Roger. She was killed about a year ago. Her picture was in the newspapers. My paper had a big picture of her. That's how I recognized her tonight.'

'I don't remember anything about it.'

'No,' said Bill. 'Why should you? But I'm a newspaper man. Newspaper men remember these things. Kathleen Henson lived with her father and mother in a house in Monmouth Road. One night, she was going to a dance with her boyfriend. He had not arrived when she was ready. So she went into the street to wait for him.' Again, he stopped speaking.

'Well? What happened? Go on, Bill, please!'

'Nobody can be quite sure. She stood there and she waited. A car came down Monmouth Road. She thought it was her boyfriend's car. She ran into the street. She thought that the car would stop. It didn't. The driver was a stranger. He didn't know that she was waiting for somebody else. He didn't know that she thought his car would stop. He didn't slow down. He couldn't. It was too late. He ran over her. She was killed.'

'What a terrible thing!' cried Roger's wife.

'Yes,' said Bill. 'It was. The police decided that it was an accident. They didn't blame the driver. My newspaper sent me to Monmouth Road. I asked a lot of questions but I couldn't discover any new facts. Now you know why I recognized the girl. I have never forgotten her.'

'But, Bill, why did Kathleen Henson speak to *me*? Why did she command *me* to drive down Monmouth Road?'

'It was your car that killed her. Take my advice, Roger. Don't ever drive that car again.'

A friend of the family

'I know you won't like it, but we can't refuse.'

Cecily Frobisher passed a letter to her husband while she spoke. They were sitting at the breakfast table in their big, comfortable kitchen. The postman had just delivered their letters.

'Read it for yourself, Frederic,' she said. 'Then you'll see how difficult it is. I have been Susan Blake's friend for more than twenty years. We were at school together. How *can* I refuse to let her daughter come to stay with us?'

'I know you're fond of Susan. I like her, too. But I don't like that husband of hers. He's a terrible fellow. I don't trust him. He tells lies.'

'I don't like him, either. Nor do I trust him. But Terence Blake isn't coming here to stay. Nor is Susan. It's Isobel, their daughter, who is coming. *Please* read the letter, Frederic. Then you'll understand. And I hope you'll agree with me that she must come.'

Frederic Frobisher began to read Susan Blake's letter. It was a long one, but he read it all very carefully. He wanted to help his wife if he could.

Susan had explained her problem clearly. Her husband, Terence, had got a job in Canada. It was a well-paid job and they needed the money. He had gone to Canada already, and she wanted to join him there as soon as possible. But Isobel was only sixteen and she was still at school. Her mother wanted her to remain at school in England until she was eighteen. Then she was going to join her mother and father in Canada. Susan wanted Isobel to live with the Frobishers until she left school. Susan and Cecily were old friends. Susan would be happy about Isobel if Cecily looked after her. If Cecily could not agree to do this, Susan would not go to Canada. The Frobishers were the only real friends that she had. Isobel's grandparents were all dead. So, where else could Isobel go?

Frederic Frobisher passed the letter back to his wife.

'I'm sorry for her,' he said.

'So am I, Frederic. She *must* join Terence as soon as she can. This is the first good job he's had for years.'

'And if she doesn't join him, he'll do something silly. He'll lose the job. I tell you, he can't be trusted. His wife doesn't trust him.'

'That's not Susan's fault,' his wife said.

'She'd be a fool if she did trust him!' Frederic answered angrily. 'He wasn't honest when he sold us this house.'

'That was ten years ago,' Cecily reminded him gently. 'And we've been very happy here.'

He smiled at her. 'We've always been happy, my dear. We've been happy together in all the houses we've lived in. And this *is* a lovely house. But Terence Blake told lies about it and he charged us far too much for it.'

'Perhaps he was sad. Perhaps he didn't want to sell it. His family had lived here for many, many years. His father and mother—Isobel's grandfather and grandmother—lived here. Blakes have lived here for hundreds of years. Of course he didn't want to sell it.'

'That was his fault. He had been careless and foolish. He had spent all his money. He *had* to sell the house. He couldn't afford to live here any longer.'

Cecily got out of her chair. She put her hand on her husband's arm.

'Don't talk about Terence any more, dear. I agree with you about him. But what shall I tell Susan?'

Frederic Frobisher was quiet for a moment. Then he said slowly, 'I've told you already, Cecily, I'm sorry for Susan. I'd like to help her.'

'Then shall I write to her and tell her that Isobel may come?'

Her husband looked at his watch. 'It's late,' he said. 'I ought to have started work half an hour ago.' He turned to his wife.

'You'd like the girl to come here, wouldn't you?' he asked.

She nodded. 'Yes, Frederic. I haven't seen Isobel for a long time, but she was a nice little girl. It will be fun to have her with us. After all, she is a friend of the family.'

Frederic smiled. 'Write today, Cecily. Invite her to come. We'll try to make her happy.'

He left the kitchen and closed the door behind him. She heard his footsteps crossing the hall. Then she heard his library door open and close. He was writing a new book and he would not leave his desk until lunchtime.

'Oh well,' she said to herself, 'Isobel won't be a trouble to him. She won't be in the way. The house is big. There's plenty of room for us all.'

About a month later, on a dark December evening, Cecily Frobisher stood in the hall alone. Her husband had driven his car to the railway station. He had gone to meet Isobel Blake's train. She looked round the hall. A cheerful fire was burning and all the lights were turned on. She wanted the house to welcome Isobel. She ran upstairs to make sure that the girl's bedroom was warm and bright.

When she came downstairs again she suddenly felt ill. Her heart was beating hard and her head was hurting her. She sat down in a chair beside the fire.

'Cecily Frobisher,' she said to herself, 'you are a foolish woman. You are nervous. You are nervous because a sixteen-year-old girl is coming to stay with you. What a silly woman you are! Why are you afraid? You have a loving husband who earns a lot of money. He writes important books that thousands of people buy. You are well and happy. Now, close your eyes and rest until Isobel arrives.'

She fell asleep in her comfortable chair by the warm fire. She fell into a deep sleep and she dreamed. In her dream she could see the hall. She could see herself asleep in the chair. And she saw the library door open. An old woman came through the door. She was wearing a long black dress and her hair was white. She walked slowly across the hall and stopped by the fire. She turned her face to the sleeping woman. And Cecily knew that her strange visitor was going to speak.

'Don't!' Cecily cried out. 'Don't speak! Don't speak to me! I won't listen to you!'

Her own shout woke her. She sprang to her feet. The hall was empty. Then the front door opened and she heard a girl's voice.

'I know the way in. I used to live here, you know. I could walk about this house in the dark.'

Frederic and Isobel came towards her. He was carrying the girl's case and smiling.

'Here we are, Cecily. The train was late. It's a cold, wet night. Take Isobel up to her room. I'll bring her case up. Then we'll have dinner. I'm hungry. I'm sure Isobel is ready for a meal.'

Isobel was tall, dark and rather thin. Her eyes were bright and she was breathing quickly. But she was not nervous. Oh no, Cecily was sure that the girl was not nervous. She was excited and she spoke quickly, but she had no fear.

'Mrs Frobisher,' she said, 'it's good of you to let me come here. I have come home again, you know.'

Her words were polite. Cecily tried to answer them, but she felt uncomfortable. She felt strange in her own house. Was this girl the visitor or was she?

Isobel looked round the hall. 'It's different,' she said. 'You've made changes.'

'Well, we've——' But Cecily was not allowed to explain.

'Of course, it's full of light and it's warm. We never had a fire in the hall. We couldn't afford it. But you are rich, aren't you?'

'No,' said Cecily—she tried to speak quietly—'No, Isobel, we are *not* rich. We have enough——'

'Which room have you given me?' Again, she did not

wait to hear Cecily's words.

'You will be sleeping in the big front bedroom. It has a lovely view of the garden. I thought you'd like——'

'Yes. Thank you. That always was *my* room. Don't come up with me. I know the way.'

And she ran up the stairs. Frederic followed slowly, with her case in his hand. Cecily stood and watched them go.

When Frederic returned to the hall, his wife was staring into the fire. He came towards her and she turned round.

'I've made a great mistake, Frederic.'

'Oh, it's too soon to say that. Everything's rather strange. We are used to a quiet life. It'll be all right.'

He was trying to give her comfort, but he spoke nervously. His voice was so quiet that she could hardly hear him.

A week passed and Cecily became more hopeful. Perhaps she had not made a mistake, after all. Isobel was very little trouble. She helped with the cooking. She joined politely in the conversation at meals and in the evening. She went to bed early and she was often upstairs in her own room. But she seemed happy in her new life.

'I'm afraid you must be lonely,' Cecily said to her one day. They were in the kitchen. Lunch was nearly ready. 'It will be better for you when the holidays end. You will make friends of your own age when you go to your new school. It's a lonely life for a young girl in this big house.'

'Lonely!' Isobel smiled at her. 'I'm not lonely, Mrs Frobisher. I can't be lonely here.'

'That's kind of you, my dear.' Cecily was pleased. Perhaps Isobel was becoming fond of them. 'But you do need friends of your own age. You'll be able to invite young people here when you make friends at school.'

'I don't need any young friends. The friends I need are here already.'

'Yes, dear, it's nice of you to say that. But Frederic and I are much too old to be——'

'Oh, I wasn't thinking of you and your husband.'

'What *do* you mean, Isobel? Who——?'

The girl left the room before Cecily could finish her question. The door closed behind her and Cecily heard her laugh softly as she crossed the hall.

After supper that night, Frederic and Cecily Frobisher sat by the fire in the hall. Isobel had gone upstairs to her room. They sat quietly. They wanted to talk to each other, but they could not find the words.

Cecily spoke first. She spoke very quietly. She was afraid to speak loudly.

'You don't look well, Frederic. What's the matter? Aren't you pleased with your new book?'

'It's difficult to explain, Cecily. It's silly of me, I know. But I haven't been able to write since Isobel came to live with us.'

'But she doesn't trouble you, does she? She doesn't make a noise. I sometimes think that she is too quiet.'

'Oh no, *she* doesn't trouble me. It's not Isobel who——' He stopped. He seemed to be afraid.

'Go on, Frederic. Tell me. Please tell me.'

'Well, you know that I must be alone when I am writing a book. I cannot work unless I am quiet and alone. That is why my library is so important to me. It is big and quiet and comfortable. My books are there. I can sit at my desk and write for hours.'

'I know, dear. But nothing has changed. Your library is the same as it always was. You go in there every morning after breakfast and you stay there until lunch.'

'Yes. And I have not written anything. Oh, I have tried. I have tried hard. But I cannot think about my work. I'm not alone in there.'

'Not alone! What *do* you mean, Frederic? I never come into the library when you are busy. I'm sure Isobel doesn't. If she does, you must tell her not to. Or I will tell her.'

'No. *She* hasn't been in. But when I sit in my writing chair I can hear a voice. I think it's a woman's voice—an old woman's voice. She seems to be saying something to me, but I can't hear the words. The room seems strange to me. It doesn't seem to belong to me. My desk is not mine. My chair is not mine. Nothing in my library is mine.'

'Frederic! Stop!'—Cecily's voice rose—'You are making me afraid. You need a rest—a holiday. We must——'

She stopped speaking. A shadow fell across her face. She looked up. Isobel was standing on the stairs.

'What do you want? Why do you move so quietly?' Fear made her voice angry.

'I always move quietly,' the girl answered. She seemed to be smiling at them. 'You like the house to be quiet. I try not to be a trouble to you. I was thirsty. I came down to get a glass of water.'

'Then get it and go back to your room.'

'Yes, Mrs Frobisher.'

A moment later she returned from the kitchen. She put the glass down and stood between them.

'Neither of you ever saw my grandmother, did you?'

'I didn't,' Frederic answered, 'and I don't think my wife did. We didn't visit this house when you lived here. Your mother came to stay with us once or twice, but we didn't come here.'

'My grandmother lived here with us when I was a little girl. I loved her very much. She told me a lot of stories about the house. It's very ancient, you know. She died here. Soon after that, my father lost his money and you bought our house.'

'It was very sad for you, Isobel. We are sorry for you, but——'

'Oh, don't be sorry for me. I'm back now. My grandmother promised me that the house would be mine.'

Isobel smiled at them again. Nobody spoke for a minute or two. Then she said, 'I hope that I shall be allowed to use your library, Mr Frobisher. It used to be my grandmother's own, special room. She did not like anybody else to use it. Except me. She liked me to sit in there with her. I used to sit there and listen to her stories. If I come into the room I shall be very quiet. I was always quiet when she was talking to me.'

'But. . . I don't think. . . no. . . it wouldn't. . .' Frederic's voice died away. He glanced across at his wife. Her hands were covering her face.

'Don't try to decide now. You can give me your answer in the morning. I must go to bed now. Oh, I nearly forgot. Here is a photograph of my grandmother. I brought it downstairs with me. I'm sure it will interest you, Mrs Frobisher.'

Isobel pushed the photograph into Cecily's hands. 'Look at it,' she said. 'You may recognize it, after all.'

Cecily's face went white and her cry of fear rang through the quiet room. She *had* recognized the photograph. It was a picture of the old woman she had seen in her dream.

Neither of the Frobishers slept that night. They lay in bed and talked in quiet voices.

'What *can* we do, Frederic? She must go away. She's driving us out of our house.'

'She's not going to drive me out.'

'But she's not alone. That terrible old woman is here. She's helping her. Don't you remember what Isobel said? She told us that her grandmother promised her the house. She'll take it away from us.'

'That's impossible. It's our house. We bought it. And how *can* the old woman be here? She's dead.'

'Well, explain to me why you are not alone in the library. Who is in there with you? Why did I recognize that photograph?'

'But, Cecily——'

'Sh! Listen!'

They heard the library door open. Then it closed. Slow footsteps crossed the hall. Somebody—or something—climbed the stairs. They heard the footsteps go past their bedroom door. Then Isobel's bedroom door opened and closed. And, in the distance, in the darkness, they could hear voices.

Cecily took her husband's hand. 'Take me away tomorrow, Frederic. I am afraid.'

'We'll go tomorrow morning, my dear. But Isobel must come with us. We can't leave her here alone.'

As soon as it was light, Frederic dressed. 'Pack a case,' he said. 'We can stay at the hotel in the village for a day or two. I'll wake Isobel. Then I'll make a pot of tea and we'll start.'

Before Cecily was ready he was back. 'Hurry!' he said. 'Leave that case. Isobel isn't in her room.'

'Not in her room! Where is she?'

Frederic hurried his wife downstairs and out of the house before he answered.

'The library door is locked. I can't get in. But Isobel is in there. And she's talking to someone.'

He drove to the village and left Cecily at the hotel.

'You'll be safe here. Wait until I return.'

'Where are you going, Frederic?'

'I'm going to fetch a policeman and the doctor. Then I'm going back to our house—if it *is* our house.'

'I shall have to break a window and climb in,' the policeman said. 'That lock is too strong to break.'

Frederic Frobisher and the doctor waited at the library door. They heard the window glass break. Then the key was turned and the door opened.

'You'd better come in, doctor. No, not you, Mr Frobisher. It's nasty in there.'

Frederic's heart beat quickly. He heard noises in the library. The policeman spoke. A chair was moved. The

61

doctor said something. The minutes seemed like hours.

Then the library door opened again and the doctor came out. He took Frederic's arm and led him to a chair at the other end of the hall.

'She's dead, Mr Frobisher. She's sitting in the big writing chair. How old did you say she was?'

'Sixteen, doctor. She had her sixteenth birthday just before she came to live with us.'

'Sixteen! It's hard to understand what's happened to her. Her hair is white and her face is the face of an old woman.'

A birthday card for Mrs Rogers

I picked up my bag of letters and left the post office. The
bag was heavy and I had a lot of letters to deliver. But I was
feeling very cheerful. It was seven o'clock on a fine summer
morning. The sun was shining. It was going to be a warm
day.

I started on my long walk through the streets of Hillwick
with a light heart. It wasn't only the bright morning that
made me happy. We—my wife and I—had been living in
London. I had been a postman there for a long time. Then
I had the chance to get a postman's job in Hillwick and I
decided to take it. Several times I wondered whether I had
done the right thing. It is not always wise to leave the place
that you are used to. But now, six weeks after we had moved,
I knew that I had been right. We'd found a comfortable
little house with a good garden. We liked the atmosphere of
the quiet, sleepy town and we'd already made some friends.
Life in Hillwick pleased us both. I knew that we were going
to enjoy living there.

I've always liked my work. I like fresh air and exercise. A
postman gets plenty of both. I'd hate an office job if I had
one. I'd hate sitting at a desk all day.

And I think that my work is important. People need
postmen to carry their letters safely. Companies send and
receive their orders by post. The business life of the country
would stop if letters were not delivered.

But it's the private letters that I most like to deliver.
Business letters are very important but I really enjoy going
to private houses. I push the letters and cards through the
letterboxes and I hope that they contain good news. These
private letters can give people such a lot of pleasure. Old
friends write to each other. Grown-up children write to their
fathers and mothers. Boys write to the girls they are in love
with. It makes me happy to carry these letters.

The private letters cannot always be happy ones, of course. I cannot be sure that I am delivering good news. But I like to think that my work makes people cheerful. Letters do sometimes contain bad news, but most people want a visit from the postman. They like to hear the sound of the letterbox. They look forward to their post.

I was thinking of all those things as I walked down Gold Street on that bright summer morning. Most of the buildings in Gold Street were shops and offices. I delivered letters to them all. My bag was a good deal lighter when I reached the end of the street. Then I turned left into Church Road. The busiest part of the morning was over. The rest of my journey passed through quiet streets. I had to deliver letters in half a dozen sleepy roads before I returned to the post office.

Not many of the houses in Church Road had letters that morning, so I soon arrived at the last house, Number 92. I had three letters for that address. As soon as I opened the front garden gate I heard a voice.

'You have forgotten my letter, postman.'

The voice came from the garden of Number 91. A woman was standing in front of the door of that house. I could see her quite clearly over the low fence that divided the two gardens.

'Wait a moment,' I answered. 'I'll deliver these letters to Number 92, then I'll come back.'

I pushed the letters through the letterbox of Number 92, then I walked slowly up the garden path of Number 91. I searched through my bag but I could not find any letters addressed to Number 91, Church Road, Hillwick.

The woman stood there. She was waiting for me. There was a little smile on her face. She seemed certain that I had a letter for her. Her hand reached forward and I could see a big gold ring on her finger. Her grey hair was bright in the sunlight. She was wearing a dark green dress and her shoes were shining. She looked so happy that I searched through

my bag again. I did not want her to be sad.

'It may be a card,' she said. 'Sometimes he sends me a letter and sometimes he sends me a card.'

Her voice was soft and gentle. Her big brown eyes watched me.

'A card,' she said. 'A card or a letter. From my son, you know. From my son in America. He works there now. He's been away for many years, but he never forgets my birthday. It's my birthday today, postman.'

'I hope you'll have a happy. . .' I tried to speak to her. I wanted her to be happy. I wanted her to have her letter, but I knew that I hadn't got one for her.

'Please look again, postman. I'm sure you'll find it in your bag. A letter or card for Mrs Rogers. For Emily Rogers of 91 Church Road.'

I pretended to search through my bag again. I took out the few letters that were left in it. I pretended to read the addresses. I knew that I had not made a mistake. There was nothing there for Mrs Rogers, but I did not want to make her sad.

As I pretended to look for that missing letter I felt angry with her son. It was cruel of him to forget his mother's birthday, I thought. I couldn't tell her that, but that's what I thought.

At last, I had to speak. I couldn't stand there all day pretending to search for her letter. I had my work to do. I had to return to the post office.

'I'm sorry, Mrs Rogers. There's nothing here for you. Perhaps there will be a letter or a card later today. Perhaps . . .perhaps tomorrow. . .I'm sorry. . .I must. . .'

The happy smile had gone and I saw tears in her eyes. Suddenly, she looked very small and very old.

'You are ill,' I said. 'Let me help you into the house.'

'No,' she said. 'No.' Her voice was very weak. 'No,' she said again. 'I don't matter. It's my son. . .my dear son. Something has happened to him. He has never forgotten before.'

She turned away from me. I walked slowly down the garden path. When I reached the gate I looked back. The front door of Number 91 was closing and Mrs Rogers had disappeared.

I delivered the rest of the letters and cards in my bag and I returned to the post office. I had finished my morning's work. I was free until six o'clock that evening. At that time I had to return to the post office. It was my duty to take the letters posted in Hillwick to the railway station. There, I had to put them on the train. But I was free for some hours. I was going home to have a rest. Then I was going to do some work in my garden.

I started to ride my bicycle down Sheep Street but I did not go far. I stopped at a little restaurant and I went in and ordered a cup of coffee. I didn't specially want the coffee, but I did want to think. So I sat at a table in the sunny window. I stared out at the people in the street and my coffee went cold.

I couldn't keep my thoughts away from Mrs Rogers. I had been thinking about her all morning. Poor woman! I could still see the tears in her eyes. What a sad birthday for her! And she had been so excited when she was waiting for me. My visit had made her terribly unhappy. It wasn't my fault, of course. I blamed her son. He had forgotten her birthday. He had made her sad. He had been careless. No, he had been worse than careless—he had been cruel.

But I couldn't forget her sad face. I blamed her son but that didn't help Mrs Rogers. It was his fault, I knew, but she was still unhappy. What could I do?

Then, I had an idea. Perhaps it wasn't a very clever idea, but it was the best that I could think of. I left my cold coffee on the table and I rushed out into the street. I rode into Gold Street as quickly as I could. I went to a newspaper shop where they sold picture postcards and birthday cards and I chose a card for Mrs Rogers.

I chose the birthday card very carefully. It wasn't easy to find a suitable one. Many of the cards were suitable only for children. Most of the cards for grown-ups were unsuitable for Mrs Rogers. At least, I thought they would be unsuitable for her. I didn't know her well, of course. I had seen her only once. Yes, I had seen her for the first time only that morning, but I was sure that she was a sensible woman. Her son's unkindness had made her very sad, but I could understand that. The way she dressed and the way she spoke showed that she was sensible.

I knew that she would not like the funny birthday cards. Well, they *tried* to be funny, but they didn't make me smile. They wouldn't make Mrs Rogers smile, either. The best of them were silly and the worst were nasty. And the birthday cards with animals on the front were just as bad. I got tired of looking at cats and dogs and horses in ugly colours. The photographs and drawings were terrible. The animals weren't like real animals. Some of them were dressed in clothes. Laughing cats!...Crying dogs!...Talking horses! ...Ugh! I couldn't give Mrs Rogers one of those.

At last I found a birthday card that I liked. It was a copy of a picture by Turner, the great English painter. The colours were good. Inside, there was a plain message: 'Happy Birthday'—that was all.

Below the message I wrote: 'For Mrs Rogers. I hope that I shall bring you a card from your son tomorrow.' Then I signed my name and added, 'Your Postman.'

I felt better when I had done that. Mrs Rogers was going to have a birthday card, after all. Of course, a birthday card from a stranger was not like a birthday card from her son. I knew that. I could not make her as happy as he could. But *he* hadn't sent her a card on her birthday. I was going to. At least, she would know that somebody was thinking about her. She would not feel as sad as she had felt.

I rode my bicycle down Gold Street. At the bottom I

turned left into Church Road. A big lorry was parked outside one of the houses. The traffic could not move. I had to wait. It was going to be a slow trip to Number 91.

I thought over the day's problems while I waited. Why was I taking so much trouble? I could be at home now. I could be at work in my garden. Why was I trying to look after Mrs Rogers? Why hadn't I seen her until she spoke to me today? After all, I had been working in Hillwick for six weeks. I had been delivering letters in Church Road for six weeks. But there had not been any letters for Number 91. I had not delivered anything to that address. I had not seen Mrs Rogers at her door—or in her garden—or at her garden gate.

I thought that it was strange, but I had no answer to the problem. The traffic began to move. I rode on towards Mrs Rogers's house.

I got off my bicycle at her garden gate. While I walked up the garden path, I tried to solve another problem.

I asked myself, 'Shall I push the card through the letterbox and walk away?' And then I thought, 'That wouldn't be very friendly. It's her birthday. She would like to talk to somebody.'

And I wanted to talk to her. I wanted to cheer her up. I wanted to see her again. I wanted to give her the card. I wanted to put it in her hands myself. I wanted her to know that I had tried to take care of her.

So, I knocked loudly on her door. Then I stood back. I held the card out in front of me. I stared at the window and I waited for the door to open.

'You won't get an answer, postman.'

I turned round. The voice came from the garden of Number 92. A woman was standing there. She was staring at me. I had seen her before. She lived in Number 92, and her name was Sparson. I had seen her glance at me through her window when I was delivering letters.

I didn't want to talk to her but I had to. She seemed to

know something about Mrs Rogers.

'I don't understand——' I said.

'I tell you, postman, you won't get an answer.'

'But I've got a card here for Number 91.'

'That house is empty,' she said.

'I've got a card,' I said again. 'I've got a birthday card for Mrs Rogers. It's her birthday today.'

'I know it is,' she said. 'At least, I know it *was*.'

'Was?' I asked. 'What do you mean?'

'I mean that Number 91 is empty. I mean that Mrs Rogers doesn't live there. Nobody lives there. Nobody has lived there for the past year.'

'But I saw Mrs Rogers this morning.'

'You were dreaming,' said Mrs Sparson.

'She was waiting for me. She told me that it was her birthday. She was hoping to have a card from her son. He lives in America.'

'He *used* to live in America.' Mrs Sparson's voice seemed louder. 'Listen, postman. A year ago today, Mrs Rogers was waiting for a birthday card from her son. He never forgot her birthday. The card didn't arrive, but later that day a telegram was delivered to Number 91. It told her that her son was dead. He had been killed in a car accident.'

'Poor Mrs Rogers!' I said. 'What terrible news! And on her birthday, too! It was a terrible message to receive on her birthday.'

'It was,' said Mrs Sparson. 'She died that evening. She died on her birthday, a year ago. She died of a broken heart.'

I stood quite still for a moment. Mrs Sparson stared at me. Then she walked towards her door.

'I can't stand here all morning,' she said. 'I've got work to do.'

I heard her shut her door. I put Mrs Rogers's birthday card in my pocket and I walked slowly towards the garden gate.

Exercises in Comprehension and Structure

Oldcastle Hill
Use —*ing* forms and any other necessary words to complete these sentences about the story *Oldcastle Hill*.
1. Mr Robinson was fond of...
2. Mrs Wills liked...
3. Halfway down the hill, Mr Robinson felt somebody...
4. Mr Robinson fell without...
5. The detective was glad to see men...

Room 7
Complete these sentences. We have done Number 1 for you.
1. It was too dangerous to *stay on the main road*.
2. It wouldn't be safe to...
3. Mrs Richards said that it was no trouble to...
4. It wouldn't be fair to...
5. Mrs Richards said that it had been a pleasure to...
6. It made Mrs Richards sad to...

The doctor's last visit
Complete the sentences in the way that we have completed Number 1.
1. *If there had been* anyone else in the street, *P C Mitford would have heard them.*
2. ...lights in any of the windows...
3. ...more than one cat in the street...
4. ...a car door unlocked...
5. ...the marks of other feet on the floor...
6. ...a murder that night at Number 3, Sergeant Thomas...

Mrs Wood comes home
Complete the sentences.
1. Bill could not afford to stay in hotels because...
2. Bill had hundreds of photographs of Porchester because...
3. Mrs Wood did not go out much because...
4. It was night, but Bill could see the front of the house because...
5. Bill was careful with the photograph of Mrs Wood's house because...

The ghost in the garden

These are the answers to questions with *how* that you can ask about the story. Ask the *how* questions.

1. He was sixty.
2. About fifty miles from London.
3. It was a little garden.
4. It had been empty for several years.
5. They hanged him from a branch of the ash tree.

Roger Wingate's new car

Complete the sentences about the story. We have done Number 1 for you.

1. The garage had looked after the car *since it was new.*
2. Roger drove faster *when he...*
3. He had to switch the tape recorder on *just before he...*
4. He promised not to play the tape *before he...*
5. Bill didn't tell Roger *why he...*
6. Kathleen's boyfriend had not arrived *when she...*

A friend of the family

Report the questions in the way that we have reported the question in Number 1.

1. 'Where are you going?'—*Cecily asked Frederic where he was going.*
2. 'What shall I tell Susan?'
3. 'Why are you afraid?'
4. 'Which room have you given me?'
5. 'Aren't you pleased with your new book?'
6. 'Why do you move so quietly?'

A birthday card for Mrs Rogers

Complete the sentences. We have done Number 1 as an example.

1. The postman left London to *work in Hillwick.*
2. He went along Gold Street to...
3. He turned left into Church Road to...
4. He searched through his bag to...
5. He returned to the post office to...
6. He wanted to go home to...

Some titles in this series:

1. Recommended for use with children (aged 8–12)
2. Recommended for use with young people (aged 12–15)
3. Recommended for use with older people (aged 15 plus)
   No figure: recommended for use with all ages

Stage 4

The Prisoner of Zenda
 Anthony Hope
Silas Marner
 George Eliot (2.3)
The Thirty-Nine Steps
 John Buchan
Seven Greek Tales
 A.M. Nashif
Gold Robbery and Mine Mystery
 Richard Musman (2.3)
The Angry Valley
 Nigel Grimshaw (2.3)
Island of the Blue Dolphins
 Scott O'Dell (2.3)
The White Mountains
 John Christopher (2.3)
The Birds and other short stories
 Daphne du Maurier (2.3)
The Forger
 Robert O'Neill (2.3)
Doomwatch: the World in Danger
 K. Pedler and G. Davis (2.3)

Plays

Three Mystery Plays
 Donn Byrne
Loyalty
 Richard Musman

Non-Fiction

Oil
 Norman Wymer (2.3)
What's Happening in Medicine?
 J.H. Dent (2.3)

Stage 5

Kidnapped
 R.L. Stevenson
The Adventures of Tom Sawyer
 Mark Twain
The Sign of Indra
 Nigel Grimshaw (2)
On the Beach
 Nevil Shute
Stranger Things Have Happened
 Susan Bennett (2.3)
Mogul
 John Elliot (2.3)
Bush Fire and Hurricane Paula
 Richard Musman (2.3)
The Diamond as Big as the Ritz
and other stories
 F. Scott Fitzgerald (2.3)
The Bike Racers
 Bruce Carter (2.3)
The City of Gold and Lead
 John Christopher (2.3)
Wild Jack
 John Christopher (2.3)

Plays

The Seventh Key
 Lewis Jones and Michael Smee (2.3)
Mystery on the Moor
 Lewis Jones and Michael Smee (2.3)
Inspector Thackeray Investigates
 Kenneth James and Lloyd Mullen
 (2.3)

Non-Fiction

Animals Dangerous to Man
 Richard Musman (2.3)
Man and Modern Science
 Norman Wymer (2.3)